FIREFIGHTER HEROES

AIRPORT FIREFIGHTERS

By Spencer B...

Consultant: Beth Gambro
Reading Specialist, Yorkville, Illinois

Minneapolis, Minnesota

Teaching Tips

Before Reading

- Look at the cover of the book. Discuss the picture and the title.
- Ask readers to brainstorm a list of what they already know about firefighters. What can they expect to see in the book?
- Go on a picture walk, looking through the pictures to discuss vocabulary and make predictions about the text.

During Reading

- Read for purpose. Encourage readers to think about what firefighters do as they are reading.
- Ask readers to look for the details of the book. What are they learning about what airport firefighters need to put out fires?
- If readers encounter an unknown word, ask them to look at the sounds in the word. Then, ask them to look at the rest of the page. Are there any clues to help them understand?

After Reading

- Encourage readers to pick a buddy and reread the book together.
- Ask readers to name two things airport firefighters do during a fire. Find the pages that tell about these things.
- Ask readers to write or draw something they learned about airport firefighters.

Credits

Cover and title page, © dareon/Adobe Stock, © wellphoto/iStock, and © Dushlik/iStock; 3, © Chmee2/Valtameri/Creative Commons Attribution 3.0 Unported; 5, © kickers/iStock; 7, © ClassicStock/Alamy Stock Photo; 8–9, © Dushlik/Adobe Stock; 10, © ChiccoDodiFC/iStock; 11, © guvendemir/iStock; 12–13, © Tom/Adobe Stock; 14–15, © Captain Tom/Shutterstock; 17, © sierrarat/iStock; 18–19, © Airman 1st Class Michael Battles/Wikimedia Commons; 21, © prostooleh/Adobe Stock; 22, © Aliaksandr Bukatsich/iStock; 23TL, © wellphoto/iStock; 23TM, © Chalabala/iStock; 23TR, © John Kasawa/Adobe Stock; 23BL, © dell640/iStock; 23BR, © guvendemir/iStock.

See BearportPublishing.com for our statement on Generative AI Usage.

Library of Congress Cataloging-in-Publication Data is available at www.loc.gov or upon request from the publisher.

ISBN: 979-8-89232-718-3 (hardcover)
ISBN: 979-8-89232-768-8 (paperback)
ISBN: 979-8-89232-805-0 (ebook)

Copyright © 2025 Bearport Publishing Company. All rights reserved. No part of this publication may be reproduced in whole or in part, stored in any retrieval system, or transmitted in any form or by any means, electronic, mechanical, photocopying, recording, or otherwise, without written permission from the publisher.

For more information, write to Bearport Publishing, 5357 Penn Avenue South, Minneapolis, MN 55419.

Contents

A Plane on Fire 4

An Airport Fire Truck and Its Tools 22

Glossary 23

Index 24

Read More 24

Learn More Online......................... 24

About the Author 24

A Plane on Fire

Something is wrong with the plane that just landed.

It is on fire!

We need airport firefighters!

The firefighter heroes put on their suits.

They wear helmets, too.

Special silver gear keeps them safe from very hot fires.

The heroes jump into the fire truck.

Zoom!

The truck races down the **runway**.

It needs to get to the plane fast.

The heroes take a **hose** from the truck.

They use it to spray the fire.

Turrets on the truck spray the fire, too.

Hose

What are they spraying?

It is a special **foam**.

A plane's **fuel** makes the fire very hot.

Water alone does not work.

There is a lot of smoke.

It can hurt people inside the plane!

The firefighters go to help.

The heroes use a ladder to get inside.

They help people leave the plane.

Now, everyone is safe.

Airport firefighters must know a lot.

They learn how to help people who are hurt.

The heroes practice when there are no fires.

These heroes help so many people.

They work hard to keep our airports safe.

Thanks, firefighters!

An Airport Fire Truck and Its Tools

Airport firefighters use special trucks and tools for airplane fires.

An airport fire truck is called an ARFF.

Some trucks have an arm to shoot foam from high up.

The truck carries a lot of foam inside.

Turrets shoot foam onto airplane fires.

Glossary

foam a thick, bubbly liquid

fuel something that is burned to make power

hose a long tube that moves water or foam

runway the road where airplanes take off and land

turrets parts of fire trucks that shoot foam

Index

fire truck 8, 10, 22
foam 12, 22
hose 10
runway 8
smoke 14
turrets 10–11, 22
water 12

Read More

Earley, Ryan. *Fire Trucks (Mighty Trucks).* Coral Springs, FL: Seahorse Publishing, 2023.

Roberts, Antonia. *Firefighters (What Makes a Community?).* Minneapolis: Bearport Publishing Company, 2021.

Learn More Online

1. Go to **FactSurfer.com** or scan the QR code below.
2. Enter "**Airport Firefighters**" into the search box.
3. Click on the cover of this book to see a list of websites.

About the Author

Spencer Brinker lives in Minnesota with his family, dog, and lizard.